MW00760041

About the Author

Joanie Boney books were created to give children of all colors and nationalities a sense of unity and a sense of self-love. Beautiful Like Me, attempts to reflect the true America with its beautiful colorful multicultural aspects. In the turbulent times we live in, our children just need time to be children.

The coloring book part of the book, titled Color Story actually gives the child a chance to get involved with story and use their own imagination. Enjoy!

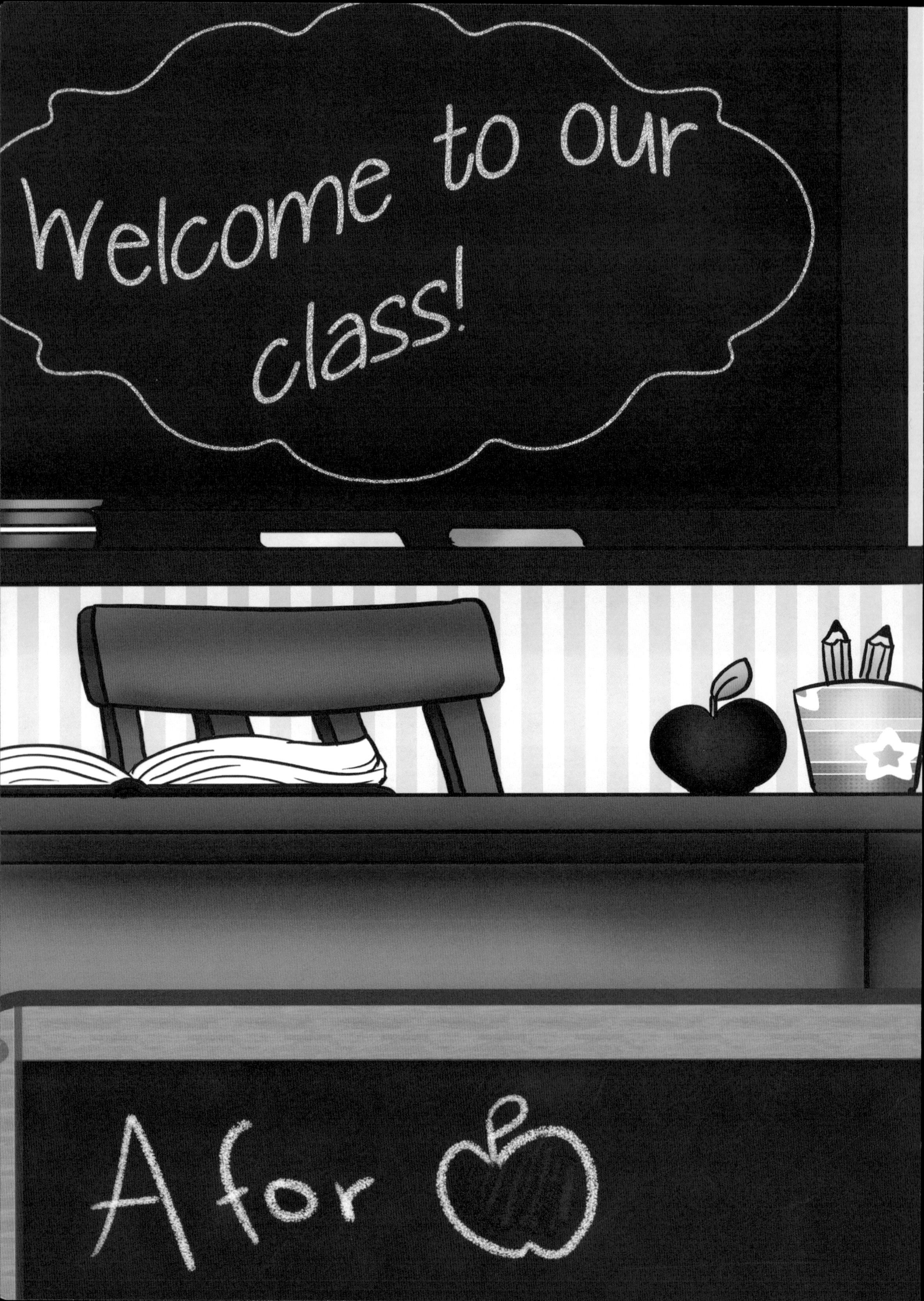
Welcome to our class!
A for

Early Monday morning Ms. Myers, the 2nd grade teacher at The Dayton School for Girls, entered her classroom, followed by a blue eyed, blonde haired little girl. The little girl held her teacher's hand and hid behind her shyly peeking ever so often to look at her new class.

"Everyone...this is Natasha... Her family moved here all the way from Russia. Please welcome her". "Come on Natasha, don't be shy, they are wonderful kids, I promise". Ms Myers said, bending down to speak to her.

Natasha peeled herself slowly away from behind Ms Myers back and walked down the aisle to the only empty seat in the back of the class.

She had never seen little girls like these before. Their skin all different shades of dark, their big brown eyes, their full lips, broad noses and their hair....wow! she thought. Their hair was incredibly different from anything she had ever seen. She wanted to touch their hair because it looked so soft.

C for 🐱

The bell rang for lunch break and Natasha followed the flock of 2nd grade girls through the hallway, and out to the playground.

There were no schools like The Dayton School for Girls in Russia. She was amazed at the different girls she saw running gleefully across the playground. In Russia everyone looked like me, Nastasha thought.

"Hey Natasha come sit with us!" she heard her name being shouted. She peered across the playground at the green tables and benches by the monkey bars. There sat three little girls she noticed from her class.

Natasha walked slowly across the busy playground;
dodging girls playing hand games, jump rope and gossiping.

E for 👁

She plopped herself on the bench beside Janice, her hair was a tiny afro, held back by a pink headband with a tiny blue bow at the front. Across from Natasha was Maria, her hair wavy and curly and Tina her hair in four large cornrows. Natasha thought all three girls were beautiful!

"Can I touch your hair?" she asked brightly hoping she didn't scare the three girls that had befriended her. "Sure!" smiled Janice. "I play in my hair all the time.

"Mine gets curly when its wet but I love when my mommy does these big twists and puts in my favorite bow" Maria added happily.

Tina jumped in "My hair is thick and gets really puffy!" she said making a ball with her two arms. Causing the other girls to giggle.

Natasha smiled. She had never seen girls so in love with their hair. There were no girls like Janice, Maria or Tina in Russia. Natasha thought to herself I like being in the United States.

The girls giggled at Natasha's fascination. "Thanks! My mommy said my skin and hair make me who I am and that I am perfectly made" Janice said smiling.

H for 🎩

Janice said to Natasha you are beautiful too, you are beautiful like me even though we are different. ""We are all different here" Tina said looking around " But we are all beautiful".

3 + 1 = 4

Natasha smiled at her new friends. They are so friendly, she realized how silly she was for being so afraid to move to America.

"Hey Natasha do you want to come over my house after school?" Tina asked. "We are baking cupcakes!" She said excitedly "Sure!" Natasha said completely free from her shyness as she walked hand in hand with her new friends.

The Beginning of a beautiful friendship.

Color Me!

Color Me!

Color Me!

Color Me!

Color Me!

Color Me!

Color Me!

Color Me!

Color Me!

Color Me!

Color Me!

Color Me!

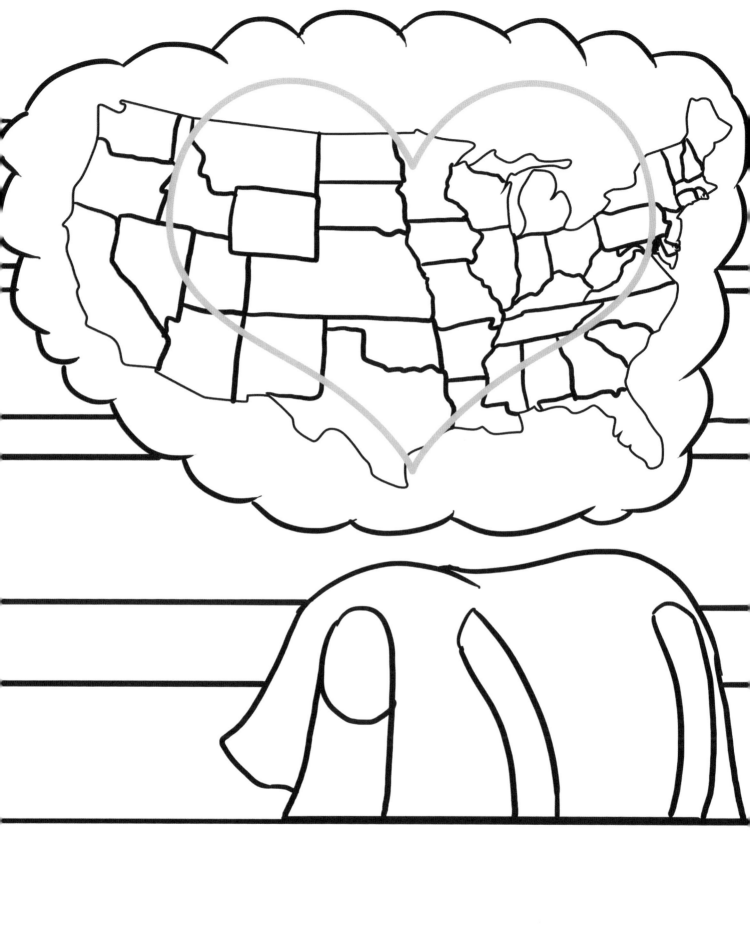

Color Me!

Color Me!

Color Me!

Color Me!

Made in the USA
Lexington, KY
19 May 2015